Contents

INTRODUCTION

Sisters Together: Move More, Eat Better is a health awareness program that encourages black women 18 years and older to maintain a healthy weight by being more physically active and eating healthy foods.

It is a project of the National Institute of Diabetes and Digestive and Kidney Diseases (NIDDK), part of the National Institutes of Health (NIH), through the Weight-control Information Network (WIN). *Sisters Together* programs are run locally by dedicated individuals or groups. Anyone who sees a need in his or her community and wants to help can start a *Sisters Together* program.

This guide and the items in the **Resources** section can help you promote the benefits of regular physical activity and healthy eating in your community. The materials are based on a pilot program of *Sisters Together: Move More, Eat Better* that took place in Boston from 1994 to 1998. These materials are updated regularly to keep them current and make them helpful for your program.

BACKGROUND

Overweight and obesity are major health problems for blacks. Recent Government statistics show that more than 80 percent of U.S. black women age 20 and older are overweight or obese. Nearly 60 percent of black women are obese. Research shows that extra pounds place strain on the body and may contribute to health problems, including high blood pressure, type 2 diabetes, stroke, heart disease, and certain cancers.

Many factors can make it difficult for black women to move more and eat better. Barriers include few stores that sell fruits, vegetables, and other healthy food options; lack of money; and limited places to exercise. These factors need to be taken into account when creating a program that promotes healthy eating and regular physical activity.

Pilot Program

To address overweight and obesity among black women, WIN and several partners developed *Sisters Together* as a pilot program. WIN's partners included Harvard University, the New England Medical Center, and Tufts University. The goal of the program was to increase physical activity and healthful eating among young black women ages 18 to 35 living in three communities in Boston, MA. Black women in these neighborhoods and experts in obesity helped develop the program. *Sisters Together* then formed partnerships with health centers, local media, recreation centers, and other groups to start new programs.

Building on the success of the pilot program, WIN designed several resources, including this guide, to support the *Sisters Together* programs across the nation in getting out the "move more, eat better" message. Over the years, groups across the country have used these resources to start and run their own *Sisters Together* programs.

USING THIS GUIDE

If you would like to start a *Sisters Together* program, this guide is for you. This guide will help you create a health awareness effort where you live that encourages black women to move more and eat better. Anyone can make positive changes. Whether you are a business owner, hair stylist, health professional, homemaker, retired person, or student, you can start a *Sisters Together* program.

The guide outlines six steps to help you plan your program and gives practical examples of activities from *Sisters Together* programs.

The six steps are:

1. Getting Started
2. Identifying Community Resources
3. Setting Your Goals
4. Working to Spread the Word about *Sisters Together*
5. Planning Activities
6. Measuring Your Success

The **Resources** section offers additional materials to help you plan and promote your program. The **Resources** section offers forms, logos, sample letters, and tip sheets that you can download and customize to print or share online with your group members. These resources were designed for black women ages 18 and older but can be adapted for other groups. As you read the guide, you will also see green boxes that outline ideas for starting up a small program when you don't have much money or many people to help out.

Feel free to contact WIN for help at any time while you develop or run your program. Our contact details appear at the end of this guide.

Let your community's needs drive how you shape your program. There is more than one way to build your program.

CREATING YOUR PROGRAM

Step 1: Getting Started

Learn about your community. Who do you want to reach?

Tailor your program based on your local needs. For example, you may find that mature black women in your neighborhood would benefit the most from a *Sisters Together* program. This program is flexible enough to target black women or other groups of all ages, races, and communities. In fact, there are *Sisters Together* programs that include men. Let your community's needs drive how you shape your program.

Gathering Background Information

Research shows that not having access to healthy foods and places to exercise may be linked with other financial, health, and social issues. When you develop your program's messages and events, think about how the community as a whole may affect peoples' attitudes and choices related to health. Then, decide on the area(s) of greatest need. These questions may help you:

- What are the attitudes, beliefs, and overall knowledge of black women in your area about healthy eating and physical activity?

- What do black women where you live already know about overweight and obesity and how being overweight or obese increases the chances of getting diabetes and heart disease?

- What types of health services and resources exist in your area?

- What types of activities are popular among black women where you live (for example, bike riding, jumping rope, walking)?

- Where can black women find healthy foods nearby?

- Who do people look up to in your area?

Know Your Community

Learn more about the people you would like to help. Gather information on age, gender, income level, race, ethnic background, language, religion, education, what kinds of food they eat, family size, and what people do for fun. You can collect this information informally by talking to local leaders and residents about themselves and their neighbors. For more formal information, you can go to the website of the U.S. Census Bureau (*http://www.census.gov*).

Get Community Input

You can get input from local people about their attitudes, beliefs, and knowledge related to physical activity and healthy eating in a number of ways. You can chat with people in person, by phone, or by email, mail, or text message. You can also host low-key meetings in your home, workplace, place of worship, local salons, and other nearby locations. Another way to learn more about people in your area is to attend meetings of other neighborhood groups.

Starting small

This guide is based on the *Sisters Together: Move More, Eat Better* pilot program, conducted in Boston by several partners. Over the years, many women have told WIN they would like to start a *Sisters Together* program, but they lacked the resources to do all the activities described in the guide. Activities like planning a community event may be too much for a program that is just starting out.

Here are some tips for starting small:

- Feel free to adapt the activities and resources in the guide to meet your needs.

- Make your program as big or small as you want. You can start with just a friend or two, a couple of interested people from your place of worship, fellow stylists, coworkers, or others in your neighborhood.

- Start small by forming a walking group with friends and getting together to share or swap healthy recipes.

- Check out the items in the **Program Resources** section under **Resources** at the end of this guide.

Assessing Your Community's Needs

When designing a *Sisters Together* program, ask yourself these questions: Does your community already have programs for healthy eating and physical activity in place? What type of program would be most appealing to local women? For example, would a program be most effective if based in a community center, neighborhood group, or place of worship? Deciding what resources are on hand and setting your program goals will help shape your plan.

Local leaders can be a helpful resource for learning more about your community. Find leaders who are trusted and well respected. Ask for their input on the best ways to reach your audience. In addition, local leaders may be able to help spread the word about your program and help you locate extra resources. Black business owners, health care providers, and religious leaders may also provide helpful feedback.

Focusing Your Efforts

Once you have a clear grasp of your community's needs, you can begin focusing your efforts. You can use the information, community input, and local leaders' feedback to figure out the best place

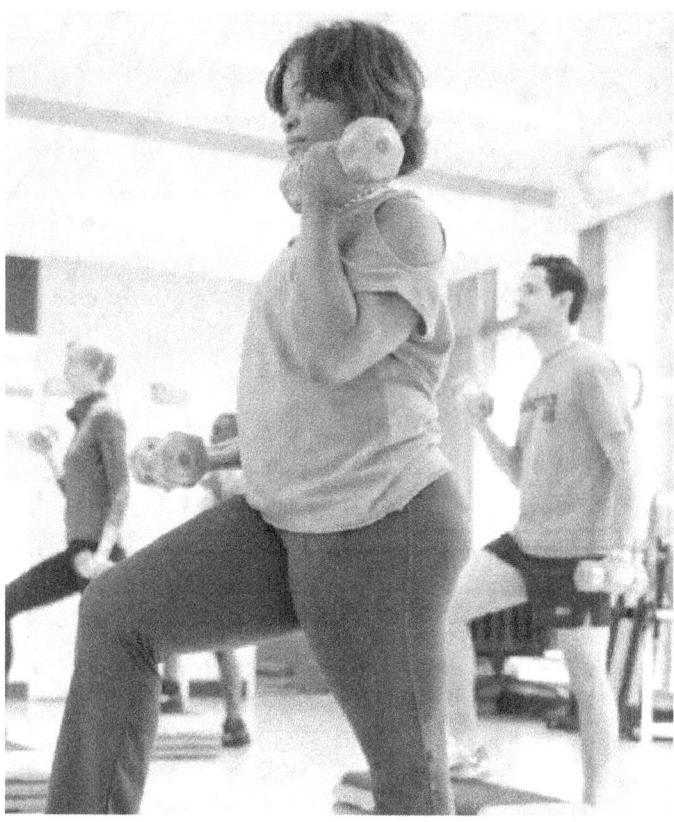

to hold your program. For example, you may decide to base your program in a community center, place of worship, or other neighborhood location.

Community Centers

A community center can be a great resource when starting a *Sisters Together* program. Programs work best at community centers when the need for information in the community is great and when the effort will most likely draw a steady following. Recreation centers, such as the YWCA or the YMCA, will often lend you their space for group meetings or exercise classes.

Find out about local groups and public programs that offer food assistance and education on healthy eating. Some of these programs are the Women, Infants, and Children Program (WIC), Head Start, and the Food Stamp Program. Check out local health centers, places of worship, social services, and sororities to learn about what they offer. These groups may serve as valuable resources when you start your program.

Sharing healthy eating tips

Here are some ideas for resources that will help kick off sessions focused on healthy eating:

- Contact the Women, Infants, and Children Program (WIC) of your county to see if it has outreach staff who can conduct a free session on healthy eating.

- Visit the "Food and Nutrition" section of the U.S. Department of Agriculture (USDA) website for tips on a number of topics related to healthy food, meal planning, and shopping. See *http://www.usda.gov* and *http://www.nutrition.gov*.

Places of Worship

Working with places of worship can be a good way to increase health awareness among blacks, since many religions have a longtime tradition of supporting community service. Before beginning the program, talk with the religious leaders to gain their support and establish credibility, open contact, and trust.

Ask for a meeting to hand out information to members, become active in events, or volunteer in programs hosted by the place of worship. You may be able to contact the director of the place of worship for ways to work together, such as being active in health fairs or using space for meetings at the site.

Neighborhoods

Is there a need for a *Sisters Together* program where you live? If so, you may find that starting a program in your area may be the best option for you. These types of small, local programs can be more personal and usually do not need many resources to start up.

Here are some ideas:

- Find out if there is a local school with a track that you could use for walking groups and other exercise events.

- Check out local shopping malls that may be good places for indoor walking, especially in bad weather.

- See if there is a local museum nearby with free or reduced admission. If so, get a schedule of exhibits or tours so you can plan a walking trip. Many museums now offer "hands-on" areas that make it easy to bring children along.

- Try holding your *Sisters Together* meetings and/or events in places like beauty salons, dance studios, day care centers, gyms, health centers, laundromats, markets, parks, playgrounds, and restaurants.

- Take turns with members in your group hosting *Sisters Together* events in your homes.

How can your community help?
What resources and partners
can you turn to?

Step 2: Identifying Community Resources

Find out how your community can help. What resources and partners can you turn to?

Partnering with individuals and groups in your community is a great way to find new members, get members to commit their time and resources, and promote your program. To find out what others are doing locally to promote healthy eating and physical activity, take note of posters and ads that convey healthy messages.

Along with other organizations and individuals already identified in this guide, possible partners could include these:

- beauty salons

- food markets and grocery stores

- local and national businesses (for donations or sponsorship to encourage people to participate, such as calendars, coupons, food items that are boxed or canned, or gift certificates)

- media outlets (such as daily newspapers, local and national magazines, radio and TV stations, and websites)

- neighborhood associations and housing authorities

- schools

- sororities

You should also consider other local resources, such as biking trails, existing parks, hiking trails, soccer fields, and walking paths that could be used for *Sisters Together* activities.

Selecting Partners

Begin by creating a list of individuals and groups most likely to support your program. Choose individuals and groups that do the following:

- Address women's issues and concerns.

- Are interested in and committed to improving the health of black women.

- Can contribute in important ways.

- Have access to and credibility with black women in your community.

- Use messages that are similar to those of the *Sisters Together* program.

Approaching Potential Partners

Once you have ranked the people or groups you would like to approach, think about how you would like them to support your *Sisters Together* program. Match your program needs with their interests and develop a list of key selling points that clearly describe "what's in it for them."

Finding partners

Not sure where to start? Here are some ideas:

- Think about other people and groups in your area that share common values and interests with *Sisters Together*. These could be community centers, health care providers, local places of worship, salon owners, schools, and women's groups.

- Create a small, core group of people who want to work with you to get the program started. Together, think about possible activities, participants, and partners.

- Consider planning a kickoff meeting to introduce the program to others in the community.

Resources in this guide you can use

- Contacts List
- Planning an Informational Meeting
- Sample Recruitment Flyer
- *Sisters Together* Fact Sheet

The following steps may help you enlist a partner:

- Call, email, or write your contact and explain that you would like to discuss a potential partnership opportunity that might be of interest to him or her. Describe the goals and potential benefits of your program. Request a meeting to discuss the possibility further.

- Have a "pitch" or notes ready when you approach possible partners. You can start your talk with information about the health benefits of moving more and eating better and the health risks of being overweight and inactive. See WIN's fact sheet *Do You Know Some of the Health Risks of Being Overweight?* (*http://win.niddk.nih.gov/ publications/PDFs/hlthrisks1104.pdf*).

- Share a copy of the *Sisters Together* fact sheet included in this guide. You can also use the *Sisters Together* logo for the letters you send.

- Be prepared to offer something in return, such as attracting media attention, displaying the partner's logo, or presenting awards.

- Ask for a commitment, but be aware that your potential partner will probably need time to review your request.

After your first meeting, follow up quickly with a thank you by email or letter that states your interest again in being partners. Prompt your contact to get in touch with you if there are any questions. Once you have agreed to partner, do the following:

- Try to assign one person in your *Sisters Together* group as the main contact for that partner.

- Consider putting your agreement in writing (perhaps a letter signed by you and the partner that describes the purpose of the partnership and what each partner will do).

- Update your partner regularly. Use the partner's feedback to refine your program. This advice can help you attract new members and help you decide where to promote your events.

- Do not forget to say thank you with letters, certificates, or public recognition of the individual's or group's contribution.

Goal: Set up 6-week walking program

Milestones	By Date	Achieved?	Notes
Hold group meeting to decide details about time and place	March 1	✓	5 people attended
Get 6 members to commit to lead for 1 week each	March 8	✓	Beth, Connie, JP, Mary, Pat, Sarah
Send out emails/ texts to group members for signup	March 10	✓	Beth, Sandra sent 17 emails/texts
Put 20 flyers up in the neighborhood	March 12	✓	JP printed and posted

Create specific goals and track your progress.

Step 3: Setting Your Goals

Plan your goals. What do you want to achieve with your program?

Creating a few specific goals will help you become more organized and plan for the future. Tracking your progress in meeting your goals can help you improve your program over time and increase the program's impact.

Try to select realistic goals. Some examples of goals that you can adapt for your program are these:

- By [**DATE**], hold a program kickoff meeting in the community.

- By [**DATE**], have a formal weekly walking program in place.

- By [**DATE**], conduct monthly meetings on healthy eating.

- By [**DATE**], have a program Facebook page started.

- By [**DATE**], have [**NUMBER**] fans of the program's Facebook page.

Feel free to adapt these goals to meet your local needs—or come up with new ones! For instance, if another group in your community is already promoting physical activity, you could focus on increasing awareness about the benefits of healthy eating, or you could partner with this group.

You may find that you need to revise your goals after you have launched your *Sisters Together* program. The needs of your community may change over time, and success is partly about being able to adjust and respond to your local needs.

Tell others about your program by using local, national, and social media.

Step 4: Spreading the Word about *Sisters Together*

Spread the word about Sisters Together. How can you get others involved?

Here are some ways to spread the word about your *Sisters Together* program.

Considering Media Sources

You can use the following media to publicize your program or healthy tips for your community:

National and Local Newspapers or Magazines (Online and Print; Monthly, Weekly, and Daily)

- calendar of events
- editorials
- food sections
- health sections
- public affairs listings
- regular columns or ads

National and Local TV and Radio Stations

- announcements of local events
- health or food shows

Online Media (Social Media)

- Facebook
- Twitter
- YouTube

Creating a List of Resource Groups for Spreading the Word

The following tips can help you create a list of media outlets or other resource groups that reach black women:

- Check with community partners and members to see if they have any direct contact or relationships with leaders in the community, local reporters or bloggers, media outlets (whether print or online), places of worship, and salon or other business owners that they can share with you. It is best if the information you gather is less than 6 months old. If it is older, you may need to call the contacts and update their information.

- If you do not have access to an existing list, begin by looking in your local phone book or doing online searches to identify media outlets and other resources for spreading the word—such as community centers, grocery stores, hair salons, and places of worship.

- Create a list or folder that includes the name, title, phone and fax numbers, and street and email addresses of contacts who handle health and wellness issues for these resources so you can send materials directly to them. Bloggers or reporters (online or print) who cover general local news are also useful contacts.

Once you have created your list, you can make it even more useful by doing these steps:

- Include notes about deadlines or events that are related to your efforts and the best method and time for notifying your contacts.

- Research the media outlets and other groups on your list. Focus on resources that reach black women first, and then branch out to various general interest groups.

Using your new list, send news and updates about *Sisters Together* meetings and events or offer short tips on physical activity and healthy eating. You might want to adapt the sample outreach letter (**Resource 11**) for community groups, local businesses, or places of worship to let them know about your program. Ask your contacts to cover or get involved with a special event, such as a walk or food festival. This not only helps to promote your program, but also helps to inform others about issues that the program addresses. When you update the people on your resource list about your events or program, remember to do the following:

Promoting the program with limited resources

If you are just starting out and don't have many resources for outreach activities, think about simple, low-cost ways to promote the program in your community. Here are some ideas:

- Focus on local media, like neighborhood newsletters and the local newspaper, radio station, and TV station. Find out who covers community news, especially health-related news. Call or email to introduce yourself and the program.

- Use the Internet. It can be a low-cost (even free) way to promote your program. Start a page on Facebook or other websites where you are a member. You can also "chat" or text about your program to get the word out.

- Call nearby places of worship to see if they will help out by announcing your program at services or putting a notice in their newsletter or bulletin or on their website.

Resources in this guide you can use

- Communication and Promotion Tools
- Sample Outreach Letter

- Send materials via email, fax, mail, Facebook, or Twitter.

- Add photographs of your group (with their permission) or other related items to increase interest.

- Allow several days for your contacts to receive and review them.

- Make a follow-up phone call to the contacts or send a follow-up email. That way, you can check that they have received the materials, answer any questions, and restate the value of the program.

- Thank your contacts with a note through mail or email for every announcement, notice, or story that occurs.

Preparing Information for Social Media

Many radio stations and newspapers now have accounts on social media, such as Facebook, Twitter, and YouTube. Remember to include all the details—the who, what, when, where, and why. When using Twitter, keep in mind that postings, or tweets, should sum up the facts in 140 characters or fewer. You may want to include a link to more information. You may also attach a photograph of a flyer, members (with their permission), or a program exhibit.

Preparing a Program Kit

For outreach efforts, you may want to prepare a simple program kit that includes information about your *Sisters Together* program and any activities you have planned.

Consider including these items in your kit (see the **Resources** section for a sample of the starred item):

- a *Sisters Together* fact sheet that describes your program and offers ways to get more information (no more than two pages)*

- any *Sisters Together* flyer that you have created for the specific event or program that you are currently wanting to highlight

- photographs of your *Sisters Together* events or members (with their permission)

- some *Sisters Together* brochures (available for download at *http://www.win.niddk.nih.gov/sisters/index.htm*)

- list of upcoming program activities

- contact name, email, and phone number

SISTERS SPOTLIGHT

Sisters Together activities at North Carolina Agricultural and Technical State University have included monthly meetings on campuses and in churches about fitness and healthy eating. Other activities have included healthy cooking events, a *Sisters Together* cookbook, and events in honor of national health days or months.

You do not need fancy packaging for your kit. You can place the items in a two-pocket folder and customize it with labels showing the *Sisters Together* logo included in the **Resources** section of this guide. You could also create your own logo. Make sure you include a place for your contact information.

Remember, too, that many of these items can be emailed or posted online. If you are contacting a blogger, online media outlet, place of worship, or other group through electronic means, you may attach electronic files or provide hyperlinks to your group's Facebook page, program materials, website, or other *Sisters Together* outreach materials.

Do not forget to update the kit yearly or whenever major changes occur in your *Sisters Together* program.

Contacting Your Resources

When you contact the resources you have compiled for your outreach efforts, stress the value of supporting black women in moving more and eating better. Explain that many black women have health problems linked to weight, like diabetes and heart disease. Note also the partners involved in *Sisters Together* to let your resources know how widespread your program is. Be sure to leave your card or name and phone number.

Once you begin contacting some groups or media outlets, they may ask to speak with you informally or to have an interview with you. Interviews give you a chance to talk about your activities and recruit members. These tips may be useful:

- Prepare well for an interview.

- Organize key message points and practice answering questions using the materials in your program kit.

- Be prepared to make simple, direct statements that are easy to understand. Get back to interviewers promptly with any promised information.

- Send a note thanking interviewers for the opportunity to talk about the *Sisters Together* program.

When planning, launching, or hosting an event, send information to your resources 3 to 4 days before the event. Make follow-up calls to see if reporters or others need more information, and encourage them to attend.

Finally, be sure to track media coverage or any response you have based on your requests or outreach efforts. Do not forget to let your contacts know about your *Sisters Together* program's successes. Community groups, online media sources, places of worship, and print media can help you promote your program and ideas. By getting the word out about successful events, you may be able to make new partners as well as further promote *Sisters Together* messages.

Choose activities that lead to healthy lifestyle changes and promote the benefits of healthy eating and physical activity.

Step 5: Planning Activities

Decide on your core activities and events. What is best for your participants and message?

Activities and events can create interest and increase awareness of your *Sisters Together* program. They can also establish an identity and highlight program messages.

Think about activities that support your program's objectives. For example, a wellness walk or bike ride may fit within your program goals better than hosting a yard sale, as physical activity is tied to your program's purpose to promote "moving more."

When planning activities, choose those that do the following:

- Address the current needs and interests of black women in your community by offering doable tips.

- Fit in with your program goals—to build awareness of the benefits of healthy eating and increased

physical activity and to provide information that can lead to healthy lifestyle changes.

- Tie in with your partners' activities and meet with your partners' approval.

- Don't need more effort, money, or time than you and your partners can contribute.

When planning activities, consider having discussions, holding meeting sessions, or providing tips to address barriers to healthy eating and physical activity. Some of these barriers—and tips to address them—are outlined in **Resource 5: Barriers to Physical Activity and Healthy Eating**. You can make copies of this tip sheet, list some of these items on a blackboard, or simply offer them up for discussion in a group setting.

Creating Promotional Materials

People love souvenirs. Consider creating *Sisters Together* giveaway items for your program members and sponsors. These items can help create interest in your program and give it exposure. Some popular giveaway items include these:

- backpacks
- pens
- T-shirts

One *Sisters Together* program made low-cost, hand-held fans featuring its program members. The program handed out the fans to local places of worship to help members stay cool in the summer. If your program has an exhibit booth, a poster or banner can provide added visibility. It can also make your booth easy to find. Consider creating a portable poster or banner to display at all of your *Sisters Together* program events.

Try to keep participants and partners updated on your *Sisters Together* program. Keep a list of the names, addresses, phone numbers, and email addresses of people who have attended your events. Call them or send them a note, text, or email to update them on future activities. An easy way to build up your mailing list is to bring a sign-up sheet to all of your events.

Planning a Kickoff Event

A great way to create excitement for your *Sisters Together* program is to plan a kickoff event. You can work with your partners to plan an event that will increase awareness of your *Sisters Together* program and its messages among the black women in your community. Some successful *Sisters Together* events have included walking groups, dance classes, aerobics classes, and cooking sessions, as well as creating a fitness calendar.

Local festivals and other venues are a good way to create buzz about your pending event. Create portable posters and signs for added visibility.

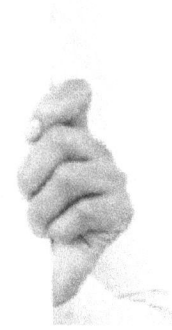

Planning your first community event

Once your program is up and running, an event across the community can be a great way to share information on healthy living and get others involved. Here are some ideas:

- Host a health fair featuring people cooking healthy foods and doing different types of dance and exercise.

- Have a recipe exchange at your salon, place of worship, or workplace. The USDA website's "Food and Nutrition" page has publications with tasty, healthy recipes. You can start with the publication *Recipes and Tips for Healthy, Thrifty Meals*, available at *http://www.cnpp.usda.gov/ publications/foodplans/miscpubs/ foodplansrecipebook.pdf*.

Resources in this guide you can use

- Sample Outreach Letter
- Sample Phone Scripts

You can promote your kickoff event by doing one or more of the following:

- Attend other local festivals and special events. Other venues are a great place to distribute your *Sisters Together* materials and create buzz about your pending event.

- Distribute flyers where you live and work. You can post them on bulletin boards at grocery stores or places of worship, give them out at meetings, or hand them out through partner groups.

- Email, text, or tweet interested members with details of the event. Ask them to send the news on to their friends.

- Invite the media.

- Put the event on your personal or program Facebook page.

How can we measure the group's success?

1. Track how many members we have each quarter.

2. Count the partners we have after 6 months.

3. Keep food diaries and discuss progress.

4. Record the number of miles walked each week.

5. Use feedback forms to find out what others think of our program.

Measuring your success will help you find out what activities work best for your community.

Step 6: Measuring Your Success

Track your progress. How can you make your program even better?

Tracking your progress can help you identify minor problems and make changes before major ones develop. It can also help you find more effective ways to publicize your *Sisters Together* activities and identify materials that best serve your community. Monitoring your success will also help you find out what activities to repeat and which ones to quit doing.

Tracking Your *Sisters Together* Materials

When you hand out flyers or door prizes, keep track of the place, date, type of items, and number of items that you give away. This will help you plan future *Sisters Together* events. For example, if you gave away all of your fact sheets at a weekend event and only a few at a weekday event, that might tell you that weekends are a better time to hand out materials.

Asking for Input from Participants and Partners

Program participants and partners can give helpful input on your *Sisters Together* program. Ask for their comments on your activities, events, and program and ask about how they were involved in the program. Some questions you may want to ask include these:

- What is working well?

- Which areas do we need to improve?

- How can we improve our program?

- What would you like the program to do next?

Ask members about any changes they have made in their lives since starting the program. Write down any comments they are willing to share with the

Tracking progress as you start out

Here are some things you can count or record to help you track your progress:

- Did you hold a kickoff meeting? How many people attended?

- How many community partners have joined the program?

- Have you held your first walking event? How many people attended? How far did you walk?

- Have you set up your contacts list? How many members do you have?

- How many brochures have you handed out?

- How many people have joined your program's Facebook page, if you have one?

Resources in this guide you can use

- Sample Participant Feedback Form

group, so you can all discuss the changes later. To have a better idea of changes that take place over time, you can also ask members to do the following:

- Track how often they do physical activity each week, and keep a weekly group count of the number of minutes/hours to compare over time.

- Track how many fruits or vegetables they eat each day.

A feedback form is a great way to find out what people think of your *Sisters Together* program events. You can use the information you gather to plan future activities. It is best to keep feedback forms simple and to the point. Try to include only multiple-choice questions. A sample feedback form is included in the **Resources** section of this guide.

SISTERS SPOTLIGHT

The Lexington-Fayette County Health Department in Lexington, KY, has been operating *Sisters Together* programs for many years. After starting up a popular initial program for women, the Department went on to start a *Brothers Together* program. Now, both programs are combined to form the *Sisters and Brothers Together Weight Loss Challenge.* A huge success in Kentucky, the program's more than 800 participants are active in healthy eating and aerobics classes. Child care and transportation support help address barriers that participants may have to joining the sessions.

Sharing Your Success

Finally, sharing your program's success with the community, your partners, and others is important. Writing and speaking about your program's success is a good way to make black women, future members, and your partners aware of *Sisters Together* and its messages. Highlighting your positive outcomes further promotes better health for black women.

We would like to hear about your program. Our **contact details** appear at the end of this guide.

RESOURCES

The materials included in this section are resources for use by *Sisters Together* programs. Each resource is available for download in a form that can be modified to suit your program's specific needs.

Program Resources

- Resource 1. Sample Phone Scripts
- Resource 2. Sample *Sisters Together* Recruitment Flyer
- Resource 3. Sample Contacts List
- Resource 4. Planning an Informational Meeting
- Resource 5. Barriers to Physical Activity and Healthy Eating
- Resource 6. Sample Participant Feedback Form
- Resource 7. Sample Certificate of Participation

Promotion Resources

- Resource 8. *Sisters Together* Fact Sheet
- Resource 9. *Sisters Together* Logo
- Resource 10. Communication and Promotion Tools
- Resource 11. Sample Outreach Letter

RESOURCE 1

Sample Phone Scripts

Potential Participants

Hello, this is [**NAME**] with [**ORGANIZATION**] calling about the *Sisters Together: Move More, Eat Better* program. This free program encourages black women to be more physically active and eat healthier. We are starting a group in your area to help black women move more and eat better. I'd like to invite you to attend one of our informal meetings. You're welcome to bring a friend or family member with you. Would you be interested in knowing the details about when and where our next meeting will be?

Potential Community Partners

Hello, my name is [**NAME**] with the [**ORGANIZATION'S**] *Sisters Together: Move More, Eat Better* program. We are part of a national program that encourages black women to become more physically active and eat healthier foods. We are planning a [**TYPE OF EVENT**] to be held on [**DATE**] at [**LOCATION**], beginning at [**TIME**].

Because [**COMMUNITY PARTNER NAME**] shares the same goals as the *Sisters Together* program, we would like to ask you to be one of our partners. To make this event a success we are asking our partners to donate [**TYPES OF ITEMS**] that we can share to promote our event in their locations. In return, we will have signs and flyers that announce your company's support prior to the event and during the event. If we are able to get media coverage, we will share your company's support there as well.

If this opportunity is of interest to you, I would love to meet with you to explain more about the *Sisters Together* program and how it can benefit the community.

Leaders or Clergy in Places of Worship

Hello, my name is [**NAME**], with the [**ORGANIZATION'S**] *Sisters Together: Move More, Eat Better* program. We are a part of a national program that encourages black women to become more physically active and eat healthier foods.

(continued on next page)

(continued from previous page)

We are planning a [**TYPE OF EVENT**] and would like your assistance in promoting this event to your congregation and community. The purpose of this event is to encourage community involvement in *Sisters Together* programs and promote the *Sisters Together* "eat better" message. We want black women and their families to embrace good health through healthy eating and increased physical activity. We believe that you, as a spiritual and community leader, can help this project come to life, through your insight, resources, and support.

Are you available sometime this week to meet and discuss this opportunity in more detail?

Other Community Resources

Hello, this is [**NAME**] with [**ORGANIZATION**] calling about the *Sisters Together: Move More, Eat Better* program. This free program encourages black women to be more physically active and eat healthier. We are planning a [**TYPE OF EVENT**] on [**DATE**] at [**LOCATION**] in [**COMMUNITY**]. I'd like to send you some information and invite you to share this information with [**NAME OF RESOURCE GROUP**]. What is the best way for me to get our program kit to you?

RESOURCE 2: Sample *Sisters Together* Recruitment Flyer

Do you want to be **active**, but don't know how to begin?

Want to make **healthy changes** in your diet, but don't know where to start?

There's a new movement in the neighborhood!

[ORGANIZATION'S] *Sisters Together* program offers lots of ways for you to *move more* and *eat better*.

Meet other women in the community as we work together to *move more* and *eat better*!

Join us on [DATE] at [TIME] at [LOCATION] as we start a new chapter of *Sisters Together*.

- Get moving with our dance classes and walking groups.
- Learn healthy cooking recipes and tips at our cooking demonstrations and healthy eating seminars.
- Spread the *Sisters Together* message by participating in community wellness walks.

The [ORGANIZATION] *Sisters Together* program was created to help black women and families in our community work together to become more physically active and adopt healthier eating habits. We host activities designed to help the women in our community because more than 80 percent of U.S. black women age 20 and older are overweight or obese and nearly 60 percent of black women are obese. Excess weight can contribute to serious health problems, such as type 2 diabetes, heart disease, and certain cancers.

SISTERS *together* **MOVE MORE EAT BETTER**

For more information on the [ORGANIZATION] *Sisters Together* program, please contact:

Name: _____

Organization: _____

Phone: _____   Email: _____

RESOURCE 3

Sample Contacts List

You can keep a contacts list in whatever form is easiest for you to manage. Here are some options:

- An inexpensive spiral notebook with different sections or a three-ring binder with dividers where you can fill in details and organize by community partners, media contacts, or program members.

- Index cards organized in a box by type of contact.

- An address book where you place information as you gather it. You can use a contacts code for the type of contact. For example, C = community partners, M = media contacts, and P = program members.

- A simple table in an electronic Word document or an Excel spreadsheet, organized like the tables below. You can add whatever type of information is important to your group. If you are able to set this up in Excel, you can make extra columns or fields so you can do a mail merge for sending group notices.

Program Participants

Name, Title, Organization	Mailing Address	Contact Information	Notes
Ms. Patty Jones Nurse Practitioner Bayview Hospital	7 Walkabout Avenue Friendsville, MN 12345	Email: pjones@cox.net Mobile: 123–444–2232 Home: 123–444–1857 Office: 123–404–3223	• Is interested in walking activities • Would like to host events at her home
			•
			•

Community Partners

Name, Title, Organization	Mailing Address	Contact Information	Notes
Maggie Smith, Ph.D. Local High School	18 Long Street Friendsville, MN 12345	Email: msmith@highschool.edu Office: 123–404–2222 Mobile: 123–444–8899 Home: 123–444–9999	• Is interested in walking activities • Would like to host events at her home
			•
			•

(continued on next page)

Download a version of this resource in Microsoft Word that you can adjust for your own program's needs at *http://www.win.niddk.nih.gov/publications/docs/ST_resource_3.doc*.

(continued from previous page)

Media/Promotion Partners

Name, Title, Organization	Mailing Address	Contact Information	Notes
Mr. Robert Washington Health Reporter *Community Herald*	33 News Lane Friendsville, MN 12345	Email: rwashington@herald.com Home: 123–444–9999 Office: 123–404–2222 Mobile: 123–444–8899 Web: *http://www.communityherald.org*	• Information must be in on Wednesday at 4 p.m. for Sunday print
			•
			•

RESOURCE 4

Planning an Informational Meeting

Starting up a new *Sisters Together* group can seem like a challenge. Where do you meet? What do you do? Whom do you invite? Meetings designed to inform others about your group and to recruit new members can go smoothly with some thought on your part. Below are some tips for how to plan and run such meetings to inform others about your *Sisters Together* program.

Meeting Planning Tips

Before the meeting

- Decide on the meeting place and time, and reserve the room. Many local community centers, libraries, places of worship, or schools offer free meeting space to community groups and may want to partner with your program to show that they care about the community.

- If you or members of your group have the means, you may want to offer healthy snacks, such as crackers and peanut butter, fruit, low-fat yogurt, or non-sugary drinks (tea, water). Ask the manager at your local grocery store to donate drinks, food, and paper products. Start early to ensure a response in time for your event.

- Arrange for child care if there may be people attending who need services. Members of your group may be willing to take turns watching the children from meeting to meeting.

- Use whatever means you have to promote the meeting: emails, flyers posted around the area, notices at places of worship, phone calls, social networking, texts, and word of mouth.

- Have current members help out, if they are able to. They can reserve the room, make flyers, contact interested people, set up the room, and get or make snacks. Asking people for help makes them feel part of the group.

On the meeting day

- Bring to the meeting:

  - Agenda

  - Pens, markers for flip charts, or chalk for blackboards

  - Refreshments, napkins, cups, and serving utensils (if you have the means)

  - Sign-up sheet (*see next page*)

  - *Sisters Together* fact sheet and brochures

- Arrive early to set up the room and ensure that all is in place.

After the meeting

- Follow up with an email, phone call, or text to attendees, if you can. If you do not have Internet services, check with your local public library, which may offer free use of computers and the Internet.

- Mention next steps, including details about the next meeting.

Download a version of this resource in Microsoft Word that you can adjust for your own program's needs at *http:/www.win.niddk.nih.gov/publications/docs/ST_resource_4.doc.*

Sisters Together: Program Sign-up Sheet

Today's Date: _____

Name	Email or Mailing Address	Phone	Comments

RESOURCE 5

Barriers to Physical Activity and Healthy Eating

As you develop your local *Sisters Together* program, you may find participants expressing a number of reasons why they don't exercise regularly or eat healthy foods. Black women who have many demands on their lives often express concerns about the impact of exercise on hairstyles, lack of support for child care, and time constraints. Other concerns about budgets, energy, not being able to eat favorite foods, and time may be barriers for some people to healthy eating. Help your *Sisters Together* members leap over these barriers with the **tip sheets starting on the next page of this resource** or with other resources discussed below.

You may use the tip sheets on barriers to physical activity and healthy eating in many ways:

- Discuss the tips at a meeting so that program members may offer support to each other and share their own ideas for dealing with these barriers.

- Make a flyer with these tips to hand out at events or post around your community, if your group has the means.

- Create a game based on the barriers. Ask group members to track points during the upcoming week when they feel they are facing one of the barriers. At the next week's meeting, discuss what barriers members faced and what they did to overcome the barriers.

- Have members exchange their own healthy recipes or discuss how they have reshaped old family favorites into healthier dishes.

Additional Resources

For more information on healthy eating plans and physical activity, use these science-based, Government resources:

2008 Physical Activity Guidelines for Americans
http://www.health.gov/paguidelines

These guidelines discuss the health benefits of specific types and amounts of physical activities.

- The toolkit combines several printable brochures, flyers, and posters in one place, including *Be Active Your Way: A Guide for Adults* (available in English and Spanish). Find the toolkit at *http://www.health.gov/paguidelines/toolkit.aspx.*

ChooseMyPlate
http://www.choosemyplate.gov

More information and interactive tools on healthy eating and physical activity are available here.

- Check out the 10 Tips Nutrition Education Series. Each one-page tip sheet has 10 easy-to-follow tips on healthy eating (such as eating on a budget or putting more fruits and vegetables into your meals). You can print these to hand out at meetings, post on a wall or refrigerator, or use as the basis for a discussion group.

Dietary Guidelines for Americans, 2010
http://www.healthierus.gov/dietaryguidelines

These guidelines provide advice on healthy eating.

- For an easy-to-read overview that you can use or print for your program, see the four-page brochure *Let's Eat for the Health of It!* at *http://www.choosemyplate.gov/food-groups/downloads/MyPlate/DG2010Brochure.pdf.*

(continued on next page)

(continued from previous page)

Tips for Handling Barriers to Physical Activity

"I don't want to mess up my hairstyle."

TIPS

- Talk with your stylist about hairstyles that fit your budget and your activity level.

- Try a natural hairstyle.

- Wrap or pull hair away from your face when you exercise.

- Get a short or easy-care hairstyle.

- Try braids, locs, twists, or weaves.

- Wear a scarf or swimming cap when you exercise.

- To remove salt that builds up in hair from day-to-day activities, shampoo with a mild, PH-balanced product at least once a week.

For more tips on keeping natural, relaxed, or braided hairstyles looking good during and after exercise, see *Hair Care Tips for Sisters On The Move* at *http://www.hsph.harvard.edu/healthliteracy/files/2012/09/sisters.pdf.*

"I don't have anyone to watch my kids while I'm active."

TIPS

- Take a family walk or plan a family game of softball or tag football.

- Dance to music with your kids.

- Take turns with another parent to look after the kids.

- Ask a family member or friend to watch the kids for a short period.

- Look for a community center or place of worship that offers free or low-cost child care.

"I'm too busy."

TIPS

Work physical activity into your daily routine:

- Wake up a half-hour earlier to walk. Schedule lunchtime workouts. Or take an evening fitness class.

- Get off the bus or subway one stop early and walk the rest of the way (be sure the area is safe).

- Do energetic housework, rake the yard, or wash the car.

- Walk to each end of the mall or shopping center when you go shopping.

- Take the stairs rather than the elevator or escalator (make sure the stairs have working lights).

- Invite a friend or neighbor to commit to fitness with you. You can encourage each other to make the time for daily or weekly sessions.

"It's too expensive."

TIPS

- Choose free activities, like going to a local walking trail, park, or school track.

- Walk around the block or the mall several times, if it is safe.

- Choose physical activities that do not require any special gear. Brisk walking and dancing are good choices.

- Check out your local community or recreation center.

- Look for workout DVDs at the library or online, and work out in your home.

- Find out if your employer offers discounts on gym memberships.

(continued on next page)

(continued from previous page)

Tips for Handling Barriers to Healthy Eating

"I don't have a lot of time or energy to fix healthy meals."

TIPS

- Try these quick, simple items for breakfast:
  - low-fat yogurt with dried cranberries or fresh berries sprinkled on top
  - microwaved oatmeal
  - whole-grain cereal (raisin bran, whole-oats cereal) with fat-free or low-fat milk and berries or bananas
  - whole-wheat toast with fruit spread
- Stock up on fruit and veggies you can eat on the run. Apples, bananas, and oranges, or a baggie with baby carrots, are easy for "grab and go" snacks.
- Buy foods that are easy and speedy to prepare, like canned tuna packed in water, pasta and tomato sauce, rice and beans, or tortillas and hummus (chickpea spread).
- Add canned, fresh, or frozen veggies (like broccoli, carrots, or spinach) to grilled chicken or pasta and rice dishes for a quick way to wake up the flavor of simple meals.

"I can't eat healthy foods when money is tight."

TIPS

- Plan ahead and cook enough food to have leftovers. Casseroles, meat loaf, or a whole cooked chicken can feed your family for several days. (Be sure to freeze or refrigerate leftovers right away to keep them safe to eat.)
- Buy store brands of pastas, whole-grain breads, and other healthy items.
- Read weekly sales flyers to plan meals around healthy items at good prices.

- Buy and split bulk items or fresh produce with neighbors or family.
- Try canned beans like black, butter, kidney, or pinto. They are loaded with protein, cost less than meat, and make fast and easy additions to your meals.
- Involve your friends by having days of cooking and sharing healthy meals together. Cut the cost of the meals by buying the ingredients together.

"I don't want to stop eating my favorite recipes."

TIPS

- Make your favorite dishes, like macaroni and cheese, but use fat-free or low-fat cheese, milk, and yogurt instead of full-fat dairy products.
- Reduce the amount of fat used in your regular recipes. Replace butter, lard, or margarine with fats that are not solid at room temperature, such as canola or olive oil.
- Keep making your family favorites, but eat smaller portions. Make half of your plate fruits and vegetables and serve a small scoop of your favorite dish on the side.
- Reduce the amount of sugar used in desserts and replace liquids with applesauce or 100 percent fruit juice to add sweetness instead.
- Make your favorite pasta and rice dishes or sandwiches with whole grains more often than refined grains. Add extra veggies, like kale, squash, or sweet potatoes, to your dishes.

RESOURCE 6

Sample Participant Feedback Form

Sisters Together: Move More, Eat Better

Please help our planning efforts by filling out both pages of this brief form and handing it in at the end of the event.

Please give us your comments or thoughts about today's event:

_____

_____

_____

How did you hear about today's event? Please check:

☐ Email

☐ Flyer

☐ Friend or family member

☐ Newspaper. Which one? _____

☐ Radio. Which station? _____

☐ Website. Which one? _____

☐ Other. Please describe: _____

What topics would you like to hear about over the next few months?

_____

What suggestions do you have for future *Sisters Together* activities or events?

_____

_____

_____

Have you attended other *Sisters Together* events? ☐ Yes ☐ No

Please tell us which ones: _____

_____

_____

(continued on next page)

(continued from previous page)

Had you heard about *Sisters Together* before this event? ☐ Yes ☐ No

If yes, please tell us how you knew about *Sisters Together* or what you heard: _____

_____

_____

Please tell us something about yourself:

How often do you get moderately intense physical activity of 10 minutes or longer (for example, bicycling, brisk walking, dancing, playing sports, running, or swimming)?

☐ Not at all right now

☐ 1–2 times a week

☐ 3–4 times a week

☐ 5–6 times a week

☐ Every day

Have you made any recent changes in your physical activity habits? ☐ Yes ☐ No

Please tell us what changes you've made: _____

_____

_____

How many servings of fruits or vegetables do you eat each day?

☐ None

☐ 1–2

☐ 3–4

☐ 5 or more

Have you made any recent changes in your eating habits? ☐ Yes ☐ No

Please tell us what changes you've made: _____

_____

_____

Thank you for taking the time to fill out this form.

RESOURCE 7

Sample Certificate of Participation

Sisters Together: Move More, Eat Better

The Weight-control Information Network

recognizes

for participating in a national program designed to encourage black women to move more and eat better.

Program Coordinator

SISTERS *together* MOVE MORE EAT BETTER

RESOURCE 8: *Sisters Together* Fact Sheet

Help Your Community Take Steps Toward Better Health

Who We Are

- Health program to encourage black women ages 18 and older to become more physically active and eat healthier foods.

- Program created by the National Institute of Diabetes and Digestive and Kidney Diseases (NIDDK) of the National Institutes of Health, part of the U.S. Department of Health and Human Services.

What We Do

- Work with groups and organizations to raise awareness among black women about the benefits of healthy eating and regular physical activity.

Why This Initiative Matters

- More than 80 percent of all black women in the United States are overweight or obese.

- Overweight and obesity increase the risk of type 2 diabetes, heart disease, and other health problems.

How We Got Started

- Pilot program developed by the Weight-control Information Network (WIN) of NIDDK. The pilot program consisted of community activities, focus group testing, materials development, seminars, and more.

TO GET MORE INFORMATION, request a program guide, or order the publications outlined on the next page, visit the *Sisters Together* web page on WIN's website at *http://win.niddk.nih.gov/sisters/index.htm* or call 1–877–946–4627.

Weight-control Information Network
1 WIN Way, Bethesda, MD 20892–3665
http://www.win.niddk.nih.gov

NIH...Turning Discovery Into Health®

How to Start a Program in Your Community

- Step 1. Getting Started

- Step 2. Identifying Community Resources

- Step 3. Setting Your Goals

- Step 4. Spreading the Word about *Sisters Together*

- Step 5. Planning Activities

- Step 6. Measuring Your Success

  National Institute of Diabetes and Digestive and Kidney Diseases  Weight-control Information Network

RESOURCE 8: *Sisters Together* Fact Sheet

Sisters Together Publications

In addition to a program guide, the *Sisters Together* program has several other publications, described below, that you may want to use with your local group. These materials are all geared to help black women move more and eat better.

You can call, email, fax, or write the WIN information service to place a total order of up to 10 free publications. You can also download and print these publications from the WIN website. These materials are not copyrighted. You may copy or print as many of these items as you would like for sharing with your coworkers, family, friends, members of your place of worship, *Sisters Together* group, and many others where you live.

To Order Publications

Call toll free: 1–877–946–4627
Fax: 202–828–1028
Email: *win@info.niddk.nih.gov*
Download:
   http://win.niddk.nih.gov/publications
Write:
   Weight-control Information Network
   1 WIN Way
   Bethesda, MD 20892–3665

Celebrate the Beauty of Youth, a brochure, explains how moving more and eating healthfully are important and help black women feel and look better and have more energy.

Energize Yourself and Your Family is a booklet that describes how being healthy and active can help give you the energy to keep up with the demands of your busy life, take better care of yourself, and be there for the people who depend on you.

Fit and Fabulous as You Mature, a booklet written for older black women, provides tips on how to get moving and eat well throughout life as you age.

Walking...A Step in the Right Direction is a tri-fold brochure that explains in simple terms how to start a walking program, presents a sample program, and shows stretches for warming up and cooling down.

National Institute of Diabetes and Digestive and Kidney Diseases

Weight-control Information Network

RESOURCE 9

Sisters Together Logo

The graphics on this page are meant to be a visual reference for the *Sisters Together* logo. Use the links provided under "Print" to download the logo in a variety of formats suitable for inserting into Word documents and for commercial printing. Use the links provided under "Web" for posting the logo onto your website or Facebook page and when creating messages to be distributed via email. The logo is available in black and white and CMYK process color. You may also simply reproduce the logo on a copy machine to add to your own flyers or other documents. A zip file containing all logo file formats listed below is available at *http://www.win.niddk.nih.gov/publications/sisters/ST_logo_pkg.zip.*

Sisters Together Logo Color

PRINT (CMYK)

Vector (commercial printer file)

http://www.win.niddk.nih.gov/publications/sisters/logo_cmyk.eps

Raster (for use in Microsoft Office products)

Large=10" wide, Medium=5" wide, Small=2" wide

http://www.win.niddk.nih.gov/publications/sisters/logo_cmyk_lg.jpg
http://www.win.niddk.nih.gov/publications/sisters/logo_cmyk_med.jpg
http://www.win.niddk.nih.gov/publications/sisters/logo_cmyk_sm.jpg

WEB (RGB)

Large=720px wide, Medium=360px wide, Small=144px wide

http://www.win.niddk.nih.gov/publications/sisters/logo_color_lg.png
http://www.win.niddk.nih.gov/publications/sisters/logo_color_med.png
http://www.win.niddk.nih.gov/publications/sisters/logo_color_sm.png

Sisters Together Logo Black and White

PRINT

Vector (commercial printer file)

http://www.win.niddk.nih.gov/publications/sisters/logo_bw.eps

Raster (for use in Microsoft Office products)

Large=10" wide, Medium=5" wide, Small=2" wide

http://www.win.niddk.nih.gov/publications/sisters/logo_bw_lg.jpg
http://www.win.niddk.nih.gov/publications/sisters/logo_bw_med.jpg
http://www.win.niddk.nih.gov/publications/sisters/logo_bw_sm.jpg

WEB

Large=720px wide, Medium=360px wide, Small=144px wide

http://www.win.niddk.nih.gov/publications/sisters/logo_bw_lg.png
http://www.win.niddk.nih.gov/publications/sisters/logo_bw_med.png
http://www.win.niddk.nih.gov/publications/sisters/logo_bw_sm.png

RESOURCE 10

Communication and Promotion Tools

You may find some tools like Facebook, the Internet, and other resources useful for staying in touch with family and friends. These tools may also help you reach current and future members of your *Sisters Together* group. Here are some ways you may use these sites to communicate with others and promote your program:

- Recruit new partners and participants by increasing awareness of your program.

- Share materials and tips on healthy eating and physical activity.

- Update people on recent and future program happenings.

Developing a Website

Websites are great ways to inform others and promote your program, but they can require a lot of time and resources. If your program is part of a larger group with a website, try adding a web page for your program. If not, consider these steps to develop a website:

1. Obtain and register a domain name (requires an annual renewal fee). Or see if one of your partners can sponsor the website or provide a page on their own website.

2. Design the website. Create a layout, find graphics, write text, and add links to help the reader move around the site. Someone in your group may have practice doing this or know someone who can volunteer some time.

3. Update the website frequently. Check often that all links are working.

Using Facebook

You can use social networking sites like Facebook (*http://www.facebook.com*) and others to set up a free and easy web page for your group. Through these sites, you can share updates with program members and partners, as well as engage potential new participants and partners. Here are some tips:

- Invite group members to "like" your page on Facebook and to ask their friends to "like" the page as well.

- Prompt fans to share news and updates by letting them know about any other social networking accounts, blogs, or web pages you may have.

- Put some hours into the site each week to keep content fresh and fans engaged.

- See the WIN Facebook page for ideas (*http://facebook.com/win.niddk.nih.gov*). You can also provide a link to WIN's Facebook page on your page.

Reference

Many of these tips are adapted from the Centers for Disease Control and Prevention's "Social Media Tools, Guidelines, and Best Practices" discussed at this link: *http://www.cdc.gov/SocialMedia/Tools/guidelines/index.html*.

RESOURCE 11

Sample Outreach Letter

The letter below is a sample of an outreach letter you can adapt to spread the word about your *Sisters Together* program.

While this sample letter targets hair-salon owners, your group could adjust it for various local groups or businesses who share your goal of health promotion. For example, the letter could be adjusted for book clubs at your city or county health departments, community recreation centers, faith-based groups, fitness clubs, local library, media outlets (on air or online, as well as print), and senior centers.

[Date]

[Name of Recipient]
[Recipient's Title]
[Address]
[City, State] [Zip]

Dear Salon Owner/Stylist [**use the reader's name, if known**]:

Are you interested in helping your clients move more and eat better? If your answer is "yes," consider joining us in spreading the word about the *Sisters Together: Move More, Eat Better* Program, a national movement that may help your clients achieve better health.

Because nearly 80 percent of black women struggle with overweight and obesity, *Sisters Together: Move More, Eat Better* encourages black women ages 18 and older and their families to exercise regularly and eat healthy meals and snacks. Overweight and obesity are risk factors for health problems such as type 2 diabetes, heart and kidney diseases, stroke, and certain cancers.

As a trusted part of the community, your business can become a **"Health Champion"** committed to lowering the rate of overweight and obesity in your area. In fact, studies have shown that beauty salons can effectively promote healthy eating and physical activity to clients.

To join in this effort, I invite you to take one or more of the following actions:

• **Read the enclosed *Sisters Together* fact sheet** [Resource 8] to learn more about our program. You can order several brochures listed on the fact sheet or download and print them to post at your business, share with your clients, or

(continued on next page)

(continued from previous page)

link to your website or blog (see *http://www.win.niddk.nih.gov/sisters/index.htm*). Discuss the tips with other stylists, salon professionals, and your clients.

- **Contact our local *Sisters Together* group** via the phone or email address listed at the end of this letter for information about our activities. You may want to join our group, partner with us on community events, or just contact us for more information that you can share with your clients.

- **Create a "Health Champion Action Plan"** that includes promoting simple, doable tips, including those from the enclosed flyer on addressing barriers to healthy eating and physical activity [Resource 5]. This plan might involve posting or promoting a **Move More Tip of the Week** one week, such as "Take a short break from work if you can to walk around the block or do some simple stretches, like touching your toes." The next week could include an **Eat Better Tip of the Week**, such as "Make half of your plate fruits and vegetables." Promote and post the tips, and ask clients to submit their own. Getting clients' ideas is a great way to keep them involved and excited about improving their health.

Lastly, we know moving more and eating better are not easy because you and your clients already juggle busy family, school, and work schedules. But the effort is worth it, and getting others in your life involved can help. I encourage you to share *Sisters Together* materials and messages with not only your clients and staff but your friends and family. Together, you can be each other's **"Health Champions"** in the *Sisters Together* Movement.

You may contact me directly at [**phone number**] or [**email address**] to discuss the enclosed materials and your interest in *Sisters Together*.

Regards,

[**Your Name**]
[**Your Group's Name**]

P. S. *Sisters Together: Move More, Eat Better* is a program coordinated by the Weight-control Information Network, a national information service of the National Institute of Diabetes and Digestive and Kidney Diseases, part of the National Institutes of Health. For more information, visit *http://www.win.niddk.nih.gov.*

Weight-control Information Network

1 WIN Way
Bethesda, MD 20892–3665
Phone: 202–828–1025
Toll-free number: 1–877–946–4627
Fax: 202–828–1028
Email: *win@info.niddk.nih.gov*
Internet: *http://www.win.niddk.nih.gov*

Like WIN on Facebook: *http://www.facebook.com/win.niddk.nih.gov*

The Weight-control Information Network (WIN) is a national information service of the National Institute of Diabetes and Digestive and Kidney Diseases (NIDDK), part of the National Institutes of Health (NIH). WIN provides the general public, health professionals, and the media with science-based, up-to-date, culturally relevant materials and tips. Topics include healthy eating, barriers to physical activity, portion control, and eating and physical activity myths. Publications produced by WIN are reviewed by both NIDDK scientists and outside experts. This publication was also reviewed by Mark Johnson, M.S.S.W., Health Equity Team Leader, Lexington-Fayette County Health Department, Lexington, KY.

Photo on page 6 and 25 courtesy of Centers for Disease Control and Prevention (CDC)/Amanda Mills
Photo on page 14 and front cover courtesy of CDC/Dawn Arlotta and Cade Martin
Photo on back cover top right courtesy of Sierra Faye Mitchell

Why should I participate in clinical trials?

Participants in clinical trials can play a more active role in their own health care, gain access to new research treatments before they are widely available, and help others by contributing to medical research. For more information, visit *http://www.clinicaltrials.gov.*